I0465070

.

The Antitrust Implications of Entry
by Small-Scale Hospitals

Introduction

Analyses of general acute care hospital mergers have traditionally defined the relevant product market as inpatient medical and surgical acute care[1] and have generally assumed that economies of scale exist at least up to 100 beds.[2] However, an examination of recent entry into California suggests that antitrust authorities should reconsider these two positions. First, twenty-one of the thirty-five general acute care hospitals in California that have recently opened or plan to open soon have fewer than 100 beds. Some of these hospitals are entering urban and suburban areas in which they must compete with larger hospitals. Entry by these hospitals suggests that sub-100 bed hospitals can efficiently provide at least some inpatient acute care services. Second, some of the sub-100 bed entrants are an outgrowth of outpatient surgery centers and provide only a subset of the services provided by full-service general acute care hospitals. The emergence of this type of hospital suggests that competitive conditions and entry conditions may now vary substantially across the range of inpatient acute care. If this is the case, then grouping separate acute care services into a broad cluster market may no longer be a useful means of simplifying the analysis of hospital mergers.

The paper is organized in the following manner. The first section describes the recent entry into California. The second section examines the implications of this entry for product market definition. The third section considers to what degree this entry should change our beliefs about hospital scale economies. The conclusion is presented in section four.

---

[1] See U.S. v. Rockford Memorial Corp 898 f.2d 1278 (7th Cir. 1990); FTC v. University Health Systems, 938 F.2d 1206, 1210-11 (11th Cir. 1991); Hospital Corp. of America, 106 F.T.C. 361; Adventist Health System/West, FTC Docket 9234, (ALJ Initial Decision, December 9, 1992).

[2] Adventist Health System/West was the only recent court case involving sub-100 bed hospitals. The administrative law judge in Ukiah concluded that Ukiah, CA would be better served by one larger hospital than by both a 43 bed hospital and a 51 bed hospital.

I. Data and Sample

Entry into the California hospital marketplace is a good subject for study for two reasons. First, because California eliminated its certificate of need (CON) program in 1987, CON considerations have not affected recent entry. Second, since 1982, California has allowed selective contracting, which has promoted price competition among health care providers. Price competition may lead to a different set of hospitals than does quality competition. If we believe that future competiton will primarily occur along price dimensions, then entry behavior in states that currently promote price competition should offer insight into future entry patterns in other states.

Table 1 lists all of the new general acute-care hospitals that have opened in California between January 1, 1989 and December 31, 1992. California's Office of Statewide Health Planning and Development (OSHPAD) groups hospitals into 24 peer groups based on bed size, service complexity, location, teaching status, and medical emphasis. The seven peer groups listed at the bottom of Table 1 account for the general acute care hospitals. The general acute care hospitals that filed hospital disclosure reports with OSHPAD for the last quarter of 1992 but not for the first quarter of 1989 comprise the list of new general acute care hospitals. Since OSHPAD requires all acute care hospitals to file disclosure reports, these hospitals represent all new entrants between January 1, 1989 and December 31, 1992. The number of licensed and staffed beds, the opening date, and the hospital location are obtained from OSHPAD's data. Table 2 lists the general acute care hospitals that have filed plans for new construction with OSHPAD's Facilities Development Division. Since plans for new construction must be filed with OSHPAD, this list essentially represents the new general acute care hospitals that will open in the near future.[3] The bed size and location are obtained from the construction plans. General acute care hospitals that will replace an existing facility are listed as replacement hospitals.

---

[3] Some of the hospitals that have filed construction plans may not actually build the facility.

Eleven of the sixteen newly opened general acute care hospitals that are listed in Table 1 are licensed for less than 100 beds, three are licensed for between 100 and 200 beds, and two are licensed for over 200 beds. Of the nineteen new or replacement general acute care hospitals that have filed construction plans with OSHPAD, ten will have a licensed bed capacity of under 100 beds, three will have a licensed bed capacity between 100 and 200 beds, and six will have a licensed bed capacity of over 200 beds. If we combine the two samples, then twenty-one of the thirty-five new or replacement general acute care hospitals are entering at a scale below 100 beds. Thus, the size of actual entry in California appears to be inconsistent with the accepted beliefs about minimum efficient scale.

We might expect to see entry at a small scale in isolated towns where demand for hospital services might only be sufficient to justify a small hospital. However, an analysis of the locations of the sub-100 bed entrants suggests that the size of most of the sub-100 bed entrants was not dictated by the size of the market. Table 3 lists the twenty-one sub-100 bed general acute care hospital entrants, the distance to the nearest general acute care hospital, and the number of other general acute care hospitals within 10 and 15 mile radii of the entrants.[4] Based on the information in Table 3, the twenty-one sub-100 bed entrants can be loosely grouped into three categories according to the distance to the nearest general acute care hospital. The first six entrants can be loosely categorized as sole providers in distinct geographic areas. For these hospitals, scale may have been dictated by the size of the market. The next four entrants can be categorized as sole providers in a suburb of a large urban area.[5] Although these hospitals are differentiated from the nearby urban hospitals by their location, their service areas would seem to overlap enough with the service areas of urban hospitals

---

[4] These figures were estimated using city maps for entrants in large cities and a California state map for entrants in smaller cities. These figures are approximate because it is difficult to pinpoint the location of some hospitals, particularly when the state map is used. Nevertheless, Table 3 provides a fairly accurate description of the geographic differentiation in the various areas.

[5] Both Vencor Hospital - Sacramento and Mercy Hospital of Folsom are located in Folsom, however, Vencor Hospital is a niche hospital, while Mercy Hospital is a full-service hospital.

so that we would not think that their entry size was dictated by the size of the market. The remaining eleven entrants, which are entering urban areas, comprise the third category. These hospitals presumably were not constrained in their choice of entry size by the size of the market. In summary, approximately two-thirds of the sub-100 bed entrants fall into the second and third categories. Since these categories describe hospitals whose service areas presumably overlap with the service areas of a number of nearby hospitals, the entry size of these hospitals probably was not dictated by the size of the market.

We might also see entry at a small scale by niche hospitals (e.g. women's hospitals). At least some of the smaller general acute care hospitals (6-30 beds) are an outgrowth of free-standing surgery centers. California initiated a program in 1988 that allowed free-standing surgery centers to provide overnight hospitalization up to three days. This enabled these surgery centers to treat the 25-40 percent of inpatient admissions that require less than three days of hospitalization.[6] Although, some of these free-standing surgery centers later became licensed as general acute care hospitals,[7] these small surgery hospitals presumably still provide only a limited range of services. Three other sub-100 bed entrants are also specialty hospitals. The San Diego Hospice Acute Care Center provides hospice care to terminally ill patients. Vencor Hospital - Sacramento provides long-term intensive care. Finally, the general acute care facility in Corcoran is being constructed to serve a prison population.

In summary, a large number of the recent hospital entrants in California have entered at a small scale. Free-standing surgery centers that have begun to offer overnight hospitalization account for some of this entry. This type of entry affects the analysis of hospital mergers because it suggests that some general acute care hospitals only provide a narrow range of acute care services. Full

---

[6] See "Post-surgical recovery-care center operators in California might seek acute-care licenses," Modern Healthcare, p. 10, Dec. 2, 1991.

[7] Id.

service, general acute care hospitals that have entered urban and suburban areas also account for some small scale entry. Their entry affects hospital merger analysis because it suggests that sub-100 bed general acute care hospitals can be competitive even in urban and suburban areas. The following section more fully considers the implications of small scale entry in California for the analysis of hospital mergers.

II. Product Market and the Likelihood of Entry

Antitrust authorities basically follow a four step process in analyzing a hospital merger. In the first step, they seek to define a collection of products that consumers would regard as close substitutes. In the second step, they consider whether the current providers of these services would be more likely to raise price if the hospital merger were consummated. Antitrust authorities then consider in step three whether the threat of entry by new hospitals would deter incumbent hospitals from increasing price. In the final step, antitrust authorities consider whether the hospital merger would enable the merging hospitals to obtain otherwise unobtainable production efficiencies. The scale and character of the recent hospital entrants in California has implications for three of these four steps: the definition of the product market, the analysis of the likelihood of entry, and the analysis of efficiencies. This section examines the implications of this entry for product market definition.

Hospital product markets can be defined in one of two ways. The 1992 Horizontal Merger Guidelines issued by the Department of Justice and the Federal Trade Commission indicate that a market is a product or group of substitutable products for which price could be increased without prompting such a decline in sales that the price increase would be unprofitable. Thus, the Horizontal Merger Guidelines approach would identify a particular hospital based service, or group of substitutable products, as a product market. For instance, twenty-four hour observation would be a product market if a substantial price increase would only slightly reduce the demand for this service.

Antitrust authorities and the courts have not used the Horizontal Merger Guidelines approach in defining hospital product markets for hospital mergers.

To define hospital product markets, antitrust authorities and the courts have instead used a cluster market approach, which argues that inpatient acute care services can be grouped together for the purpose of analyzing hospital mergers because these services are often consumed together. For example, in U.S. v. Rockford Memorial Corp., the district court judge noted "...[T]he therapy of patients who require inpatient care may require several types of diagnostic tests, twenty-four hour nursing, extensive pre or post operative observation or any combination of other services offered by an acute care hospital." The judge earlier had noted that "...[T]he core of these peculiar characteristics is the hospital's ability to provide overnight care." Like U.S. v. Rockford Memorial Corp., most hospital merger decisions have defined cluster markets to cover only inpatient services, however, in U.S. v. Carilion Health System, the district court judge included both inpatient and outpatient services in the cluster market.

Although Baker (1988) questions the complementarity justification for cluster markets, he argues that cluster markets may be a cost effective way of implementing the Horizontal Merger Guidelines when all competing firms sell multiple products or services, firm market shares do not vary significantly across products, and entry conditions are similar across products. If we use Baker's criteria, defining the product market as inpatient acute care may have been a cost-effective way of defining product markets 5 or 10 years ago. However, the emergence of small surgery hospitals, as in California, diminishes the analytic convenience of an inpatient, acute care product market since both hospital market shares and entry conditions may now vary significantly across the range of inpatient acute care.

General acute care hospital merger analysis can be adjusted to accomodate the emergence of small surgery hospitals in one of two ways. Antitrust authorities and the courts can continue to define the product market as an inpatient acute care cluster market that includes small surgery hospitals as market participants. In this case, antitrust regulators and the courts would then need to acknowledge in their analysis that the presence of small surgery hospitals, which perform uncomplicated deliveries and simple types of surgery (low-level inpatient acute care), could not prevent a price increase in more complex types of inpatient care (high-level inpatient acute care). Alternatively, antitrust authorities and the courts could define narrower product markets. These narrower product markets could be low-level inpatient acute care, in which small surgery hospitals compete, and high-level inpatient acute care, in which only larger hospitals (full-scale hospitals) compete.

Defining narrower product markets appears to be the better method of accomodating the emergence of small surgery hospitals because it forces antitrust authorities to more explicitly identify their areas of concern. To see this, let us consider a hypothetical example with the following conditions. Two full-scale hospitals and one small surgery hospital serve a small city. Some of the patients in this city go to large, full-scale hospitals in a nearby city for high level inpatient acute care.[8] Small surgery hospitals can enter without driving price below profitable levels, however full-scale hospitals cannot. The two full-scale hospitals seek to merge. Thus, the most important question in this example is whether competition from small surgery hospitals would prevent a price increase in low-level inpatient acute care while the presence of nearby full-scale hospitals would prevent a price increase in high-level inpatient acute care.

In this example, suppose that antitrust authorities consider two product markets: low-level acute care and high-level acute care. The low-level acute care product market probably would not be a concern because entry by small surgery hospitals would prevent any long-term anticompetitive harm. In contrast, the high-level acute care product market might be a concern. Because small

---

[8]   Because high-level inpatient acute care is a more expensive product than low-level inpatient acute care, we would expect that patients would be willing to bear greater search costs in shopping for high-level inpatient acute care.

surgery hospitals do not offer high-level acute care, their entry could not prevent anti-competitive harm in a high-level acute care market. Thus, to determine whether the merger of two full-scale hospitals likely would lead to anticompetitive harm in a high-level acute care product market, antitrust authorities need to consider whether the large, full-scale hospitals in the nearby city compete with the two merging hospitals in the provision of high-level acute care. If they do, then the merger would not lead to anticompetitive harm. If they do not, then the merger would be anticompetitive.

Suppose instead that the antitrust authorities define the product market as all inpatient acute care. Here, the small surgery hospitals would be included as competitors. The geographic market analysis would then consider whether the outflow of some patients for high-level acute care suggests that the full-scale hospitals in the nearby city should be included as competitors. Since the percentage of patients leaving the small city for medical care would be lower for an all inpatient acute care market than it would be for a high-level inpatient acute care market, antitrust authorities would be more likely to exclude the nearby hospitals if they used an all inpatient acute care product market. Suppose that the antitrust authorities decide to exclude the nearby hospitals from the geographic market. At this point, the antitrust authorities would then assess the competitive significance of the small surgery hospitals. Since small surgery hospitals do not offer high-level inpatient acute care, the antitrust authorities would probably conclude that the merger of the two full-scale hospitals likely would lead to anticompetitive harm in the provision of high-level acute care.

In this example, small surgery hospitals compete with the merging hospitals for low-level inpatient acute care while nearby full-scale hospitals may compete with the merging hospitals for high-level inpatient acute care. Defining two separate product markets allows antitrust authorities to directly consider to what extent small surgery hospitals can prevent anticompetitive harm in low-level inpatient care and to what extent nearby full-scale hospitals can prevent anticompetitive harm in high-level inpatient acute care. By comparison, defining an all inpatient acute care product market asks antitrust authorities to decide to what extent nearby full-scale hospitals can prevent anticompetitive harm in all inpatient acute care and to what extent small surgery hospitals can prevent anticompetitive harm in all inpatient acute care. Since, in the example, the nearby full-scale hospitals cannot prevent anticompetitive harm in low-level inpatient acute care and the small surgery hospitals cannot prevent anticompetitive harm in high-level inpatient acute care, defining an all inpatient acure care product market would have been more likely to incorrectly identify an anticompetitive problem. In our example, defining an all inpatient acute care product market could have led antitrust authorities to underestimate the competitive impact of the nearby full-scale hospitals on high-level acute care.

III. Efficiencies

Several previous studies of the minimum efficient scale (MES) for general acute care hospitals suggest that sub-100 bed general acute care hospitals are inefficient. Based on these studies, a number of health care analysts have argued that small hospitals could deliver health care more efficiently if they were allowed to attain a larger scale through merger.[9] They argue that any deleterious effects on consumer welfare from such a merger would be offset, at least partially, by the efficiency gains resulting from the merger. They further argue that, in many cases, allowing two small hospitals to merge would not adversely affect competition because one of the small hospitals is so inefficient that it would likely exit the market anyway. These arguments appear to have influenced antitrust policy. For instance, since the end of 1988, only three hospital mergers have been challenged in court by the Federal Trade Commission or the Department of Justice.[10] In one of

---

[9] For example, see Hospital Collaboration: The Need for an Appropriate Antitrust Policy; American Hospital Association; 1992.

[10] FTC v. University Health Systems, 938 F.2d. 1206, 1210-11 (11th Cir. 1991); FTC v. Columbia Hospital Corp., No. 93-30-FTM-CIV-23D. (M.D. Fla., injunction granted May 21, 1993), Adventist Health System/West, FTC Docket 9234 (ALJ Initial Decision, Dec. 9, 1992), appeal to full Commission pending.

these, Adventist Health Systems/West, the administrative law judge concluded that one larger hospital would provide better health care to Ukiah, California residents than would two hospitals with 43 beds and 51 beds respectively. In addition, a bill has been introduced in Congress that would immunize hospital mergers for hospitals that are located in cities with fewer than 125,000 people and that receive 40 percent of their gross revenue from Medicare and Medicaid.[11]

The belief that smaller general acute care hospitals are inefficient is based largely on mortality studies and survivorship studies.[12] The mortality studies (Lillie-Blanton et al. (1992), Williams et al. (1992)) find that sub-100 bed hospitals have a higher probability of closing than do other hospitals. The survivorship studies (Bays (1986), Vita et al. (1991), AHA Hospital Statistics (1992)) find that the share of general acute care hospitals that have fewer than 100 beds has declined over time. These findings have been widely interpreted as evidence that sub-100 bed hospitals are inefficient. However, the high percentage of sub-100 bed hospitals among the general acute care hospitals that have recently opened in California suggests that this interpretation may not be correct. The entry of these sub-100 bed hospitals in California suggests that, in unregulated markets, sub-100 bed general acute care hospitals may have a higher rate of entry than other general acute care hospitals. Thus, in

---

[11] H.R. 1765 (103rd Cong., 1st Sess.)

[12] A number of papers have also estimated hospital cost functions for general acute care hospitals. These studies have reached different conclusions. In their review of this literature, Cowing, Holtmann, and Powers (1983) conclude that while early studies found evidence of economies of scale up to 500 beds, later, more refined, studies have found little evidence of significant scale effects beyond small hospital sizes. More recently, Vitaliano (1987) found evidence of significant economies of scale, while Vita (1990) did not find strong evidence of scale economies. In any case, there are two reasons to question whether the results of these studies can be used to determine the current minimum efficient scale. First, as Vita (1990) concludes, even the more careful studies have limitations that make it difficult to infer the long-run minimum efficient scale. Second, the competitive conditions in the hospital industry during the periods examined by these studies differ substantially from current competitive conditions. For instance, hospitals are thought to have competed for physician loyalty by offering a higher quality of care during the time period examined by many of these studies. One component of this quality was excess bed capacity (see Joskow (1980)). Now that third party payors are demanding that hospitals compete on price as well as quality, MES may be smaller because hospitals presumably maintain less excess bed capacity.

an unregulated market, the higher rate of entry by new sub-100 bed general acute care hospitals might offset the higher rate of exit by these hospitals that has been found in the mortality studies. However, in a marketplace where CON regulations restrict entry, entry by new sub-100 bed general acute care hospitals would not offset the exit of sub-100 bed general acute care hospitals. Consequently, the observation that the market share of sub-100 bed general acute care hospitals is falling may arise simply because CON regulations prevent the entry of new sub-100 bed general acute care hospitals from replenishing the stock of sub-100 bed general acute care hospitals. If this is the case, then it would be incorrect to infer that sub-100 bed general acute care hospitals are inefficient simply because their market share has been falling in an environment in which entry has been restricted.

To examine whether a survivor analysis would yield a different result in a market where entry was unregulated, a survivor analysis was performed for California general acute care hospitals for the years 1989-1992. However, before presenting the results, we should note two possible problems with using survivor analysis to determine the optimal scale of hospitals. The first problem arises because factors other than production efficiency influence the size of hospitals. For instance, hospitals may merge in order to obtain market power rather than to achieve economies of scale. Conversely, economies of scale may only be attained at very large sizes, however, antitrust enforcement may prevent hospitals from attaining this efficient size through merger. In this case, antitrust enforcement would slow the shift of market share from small, inefficient hospitals to large, efficient hospitals.

The second problem arises because the data are imperfect for our purposes. In some cases, separate hospitals with common ownership are licensed as one hospital. These hospitals should be treated as one large hospital if they are integrated. However, they should be treated as two smaller, separate hospitals if they are not integrated. If, separate facilities have increasingly been licensed as one hospital, then a survivor analysis may overstate the market shares of larger bed size categories in later years. The data also includes the beds in psychiatric and rehabilitation units in the bed size

11

measures. If these units are not an integral part of an acute care hospital, then their inclusion overstates the bed size of a number of hospitals. Consequently, if hospitals have been adding psychiatric and rehabilitation units over time, a survivor analysis again would overstate the market shares of larger bed size categories in later years.

Table 4 and Table 5 present the results of the survivor analysis. Table 4 lists the percentage of general acute care hospitals in each of six size categories for the second quarter of 1989 and the fourth quarter of 1992.[13] The sample includes all general acute care hospitals.[14] Bed size is measured as staffed beds rather than licensed beds. Staffed beds seem to be a better measure of capacity than licensed beds because some hospitals are licensed for more beds than their physical plant can realistically accomodate. Table 4 shows that the percentage of hospitals in the 50-99 bed size and the over-400 bed size fell substantially between the second quarter of 1989 and the fourth quarter of 1992. During this period, the percentage of hospitals in the 100-199 bed size and the 300-399 bed size increased substantially. Finally, the percentage of hospitals in the 0-49 bed size and the 200-299 bed size remained essentially unchanged. These results suggest that hospitals in the 50-99 and over-400 bed sizes are relatively inefficient.

Table 5 lists the percentage of inpatient days produced by various hospital sizes. The percentage of inpatient days produced by the 0-49 and 50-99 bed sizes increased slightly between the second quarter of 1989 and the last quarter of 1992. The percentage of inpatient days produced by the 100-199 and the 300-399 bed size increased substantially. Finally, the percentage of inpatient

---

[13] No general acute care hospitals entered in the several years preceding the second quarter of 1989. Presumably, the lack of entry during this period resulted from CON regulations that were not repealed until 1987 plus the time required for actual construction. Since we are examining whether entry by small hospitals offsets exit by small hospitals, we examine a time period in which there was actual entry.

[14] General acute care hospitals are defined by the seven peer groups listed at the bottom of Table 1.

days produced by the 200-299 bed size fell slightly, and the percentage of inpatient days produced by the over-400 bed size fell substantially. These results suggest that the 0-49 and 50-99 bed general acute care hospitals are relatively more efficient than the 200-299 and over-400 bed general acute care hospitals but relatively less efficient than the 100-199 and 300-399 bed general acute care hospitals.

In summary, it is difficult to infer much from the survivor analysis. First, theoretical and data problems limit its applicability for this particular use. Second, some of the results appear peculiar. For instance, Table 4 shows that the percentage of general acute care hospitals in the 50-99 bed category fell substantially while the percentage of general acute care hospitals in the 0-49 bed category increased slightly and the percentage of general acute care hospitals in the 100-199 bed category increased substantially. If we use changes in the percentage of hospitals in a particular bed size to measure efficiency, then these results suggest that the 0-49 bed size and the 100-199 bed sizes are efficient while the 50-99 bed size is not. Consequently, although the survivor analysis provides some additional information about economies of scale, it is difficult to place much weight on this additional information.

IV. Conclusion

Of the thirty-five general acute care hospitals that have recently opened or soon will open in California, twenty-one have fewer than 100 beds. Several of these sub-100 bed hospitals are entering areas that are somewhat isolated. The scale of entry of these hospitals may have been dictated by the size of the market. Several of the other sub-100 bed hospitals are niche hospitals. Most of these are an outgrowth of free-standing surgery centers and do not provide a full range of acute care services. The remaining hospitals are full-service general acute care hospitals located in urban and suburban areas.

The entry into inpatient acute care by the small surgery hospitals complicates the definition of hospital product markets. Previously, hospital product markets had been defined as a cluster of services encompassing all inpatient acute care. This definition facilitated hospital merger analysis when most hospitals offered a similar range of services and entry conditions were similar across this range of services. The entry by the small surgery hospitals suggests that this is no longer the case since full service hospitals would compete with these small surgery hospitals for low-level inpatient acute care but would compete only amongst themselves for high-level inpatient acute care. Entry conditions also would no longer be the same across the range of inpatient acute care services. Because the small surgery hospitals can offer low-level inpatient acute care at a very small bed size, entry would be more likely to prevent a price increase among low-level inpatient acute care services than among high-level inpatient acute care services.

Finally, the high percentage of small scale entrants suggests that small general acute care hospitals may not be as inefficient as some previous studies suggest. First, some of the sub-100 bed entrants appear to be full-service general acute care hospitals entering urban and suburban areas. Investors in these hospitals are wasting their money if these hospitals are indeed inefficient. Second, the high percentage of sub-100 bed entrants suggests that, compared to other general acute care hospitals, sub-100 bed general acute care hospitals may have both a higher rate of entry and a higher rate of exit. If this is the case, then survivor studies may have observed that the share of sub-100 bed general acute care hospitals fell not because these hospitals are inefficient but rather because the studies dealt with markets where government entry restrictions prevented new sub-100 bed hospitals from replacing the sub-100 bed hospitals that had exited.

References

American Hospital Association Hospital Statistics, 1992-93 edition.

Baker, J.B., 1988, The antitrust analysis of hospital mergers and the transformation of the hospital industry, Law and Contemporary Problems, 93-164.

Bays, C.W., 1986, The determinants of hospital size: a survivor analysis, Applied Economics, 18, 359-377.

Cowing, T.G., A.G. Holtmann, and S. Powers, 1983, Hospital Cost Analysis: A Survey and Evaluation of Recent Studies, Advances in Health Economics and Health Services Research, R.M. Scheffler ed., vol 4, 257-303.

Joskow, P., 1980, The effects of competition and regulation on hospital bed supply and the reservation quality of the hospital, Bell Journal of Economics, 11, 421-447.

Lillie-Blanton, M., S. Felt, P. Redmon, S. Renn, S. Machlin, and E. Wennar, 1992, Rural and urban hospital closures, 1985-1988: Operating and environmental characteristics that affect risk, Inquiry, 29, 332-344.

Vita, M.G., 1990, Exploring hospital production relationships with flexible functional forms, Journal of Health Economics, 9, 1-21.

Vita, M.G., J.A. Langenfeld, P. Pautler, and L. Miller, 1991, Economic analysis in health care antitrust, The Journal of Contemporary Health Law and Policy, 7, 73-115.

Vitaliano, D.F., 1987, On the estimation of hospital cost functions, Journal of Health Economics, 6, 305-318.

Williams, D., J. Hadley, and J. Pettengill, 1992, Profits, community role, and hospital closures: an urban rural analysis, Medical Care, 30 no. 2, 174-187.

Table 1

List of Acute Care Hospitals that Opened between 1/86 and 12/92*

	hospital name	date opened	licensed beds	staffed beds	location	peer group
1)	San Ramon Regional Medical Center	2/90	125 beds	43 beds	San Ramon	4
2)	USC University Hospital	5/91	275 beds	85 beds	Los Angeles	3
3)	Irvine Medical Center	8/90	177 beds	177 beds	Irvine	4
4)	Menifee Valley Medical Center	6/89	84 beds	84 beds	Sun City	5
5)	Kaiser Foundation Hospital - Riverside	9/89	215 beds	192 beds	Riverside	14
6)	Moreno Valley Medical Center	10/90	95 beds	95 beds	Moreno Valley	5
7)	Mercy Hospital of Folsom (replacement)	6/89	95 beds	64 beds	Folsom	5
8)	St. Dominic's Hospital	9/90	50 beds	16 beds	Manteca	5
9)	South Valley Hospital	7/89	93 beds	92 beds	Gilroy	5
10)	St. Louise Health Center	10/89	60 beds	31 beds	Morgan Hill	5
11)	Kaiser Foundation Hospital - Santa Rosa	3/90	110 beds	106 beds	Santa Rosa	14
12)	San Diego Hospice Acute Care Center	8/91	24 beds	24 beds	San Diego	5
13)	Vencor Hospital - Sacramento	2/92	39 beds	15 beds	Folsom	5
14)	Sutter Coast Hospital (replacement)	2/92	47 beds	47 beds	Crescent City	6
15)	Patients Hospital of Redding	3/92	6 beds	6 beds	Redding	5
16)	Recovery Inn of Los Gatos	5/92	16 beds	2 beds	Campbell	5

peer groups included

1 - University Teaching
2 - Large, Non-University Teaching
3 - Large, Complex
4 - Moderate Sized
5 - Small Urban
6 - Rural
14 - Large Prepaid Health Plans

* Mercy Hospital Bakersfield (67 beds) and Valley Care Medical Center (66 beds, Pleasanton) also opened during this period. However, these two hospitals were included in the license of a larger, nearby hospital in the second quarter of 1992.

16

Table 2

Acute Care Hospitals that Filed Construction Plans with OSHPAD

	hospital name	date filed	bed size	location	
17)	Kaiser Foundation Hospital	7/89	240 beds	Baldwin Park	
18)	Sutter HealthCare	2/93	30 beds	Santa Cruz	
19)	Kaiser Roseville Medical Center	2/92	116 beds	Roseville	
20)	James P. Tate Surgical Hospital	8/90	10 beds	Redding	
21)	Family Doctor Medical Group	3/91	12 beds	Vallejo	
22)	General Acute Care Facility	11/88	50 beds	Corcoran	
23)	N.T. Enloe Hospital Satellite Facility	4/87	16 beds	Chico	
24)	San Bernadino County Medical Center	6/91	373 beds	San Bernadino	replacement
25)	Rancho Cucamonga Medical Center	12/88	49 beds	Rancho Cucamonga	
26)	Sutter Davis Hospital	10/91	50 beds	Davis	replacement
27)	Kaiser Foundation Hospital - Richmond	3/90	74 beds	Richmond	replacement
28)	Riverside General Hospital	6/91	250 beds	Moreno Valley	replacement
29)	St. John's Regional Medical Center	1/88	250 beds	Oxnard	replacement
30)	Valley Children's Medical Center	6/92	208 beds	Stuartville	replacement
31)	San Luis Obispo General Hospital	7/92	76 beds	San Luis Obispo	replacement
32)	Coalinga District Hospital	3/87	18 beds	Coalinga	replacement
33)	Merrihew Memorial Hospital	5/92	184 beds	Martinez	replacement
34)	Los Angeles Co. USC Med. Ctr.	1/93	946 beds	Los Angeles	replacement
35)	Kaiser/Fremont Med. Ctr.	2/92	106 beds	Fremont	replacement

17

Table 3

Location of Sub-100 Bed Entrants

	hospital name	bed size	location	distance to nearest hospital	number of hospitals within 10 miles	number of hospitals within 15 miles
1)	Sutter Coast Hospital (new location)	47 beds	Crescent City	50 mi.	0	0
2)	Coalinga District Hospital	18 beds	Coalinga	16 mi.	0	0
3)	General Acute Care Facility	50 beds	Corcoran	13 mi.	0	1
4)	Menifee Valley Medical Center	84 beds	Sun City	12 mi.	0	3
5)	Moreno Valley Medical Center	95 beds	Moreno Valley	11 mi.	0	7
6)	Sutter Davis Hospital	50 beds	Davis	10 mi.	1	1
7)	South Valley Hospital	93 beds	Gilroy	9 mi.	1	3
8)	St. Louise Health Center	60 beds	Morgan Hill	9 mi.	1	2
9)	Mercy Hospital of Folsom (new location)	95 beds	Folsom	1 mi.	3	6
10)	Vencor Hospital - Sacramento	39 beds	Folsom	1 mi.	3	6
11)	Rancho Cucamonga Medical Center	49 beds	Rancho Cucamonga	4 mi.	5	7
12)	James P. Tate Surgical Hospital	10 beds	Redding	3 mi.	2	2
13)	Family Doctor Medical Group	12 beds	Vallejo	3 mi.	4	10
14)	N.T. Enloe Hospital Satellite Facility	16 beds	Chico	3 mi	2	3
15)	Patient's Hospital of Redding	6 beds	Redding	3 mi.	3	3
16)	St. Dominic's Hospital	50 beds	Manteca	2 mi.	4	8
17)	Sutter HealthCare	30 beds	Santa Cruz	1 mi.	1	2
18)	Kaiser Foundation Hospital - Richmond	74 beds	Richmond	1 mi.	5	25
19)	San Luis Obispo General Hospital	76 beds	San Luis Obispo	1 mi.	2	3
20)	San Diego Hospice Acute Care Center	24 beds	San Diego	1 mi.	14	17
21)	Recovery Inn of Los Gatos	16 beds	Los Gatos	1 mi.	9	9

18

Table 4

Percentage and Number of Hospitals in Various Bed Size Categories

	0-50 beds	51-100 beds	101-200 beds	201-300 beds	301-400 beds	over 400 beds
2nd qtr 1989	0.175 (74)	0.209 (88)	0.277 (117)	0.178 (75)	0.085 (36)	0.076 (32)
4th qtr 1992	0.177 (71)	0.185 (74)	0.299 (120)	0.175 (70)	0.095 (38)	0.070 (28)

Table 5

Percentage of Inpatient Days Produced by Various Hospital Sizes

	0-50 beds	51-100 beds	101-200 beds	201-300 beds	301-400 beds	over 400 beds
2nd qtr 1989	0.023	0.073	0.208	0.254	0.182	0.260
4th qtr 1992	0.026	0.075	0.229	0.248	0.198	0.225

www.ingramcontent.com/pod-product-compliance
Lightning Source LLC
Chambersburg PA
CBHW081320180526

45170CB00007B/2785